BLOCKCHAIN TECHNOLOGY
EXPLAINED

2021

The Ultimate Beginner's Guide About Blockchain
Wallet, Mining, Bitcoin, Ethereum, Litecoin,
Monero, Ripple, Dash, IOTA and More

By

Warren Larsen

Blockchain Technology Explained 2021:

The Ultimate Beginner's Guide About Blockchain Wallet, Mining,

Bitcoin, Ethereum, Litecoin, Monero, Ripple, Dash, IOTA and More

Written by WARREN LARSEN.

Errors and Feedback

Contact us if you find any errors

TABLE OF CONTENTS

INTRODUCTION

The birth of Bitcoin in 2009, and the subsequent development of other cryptocurrencies in the following years, were the most important events in the world of alternative finance. Cryptocurrencies are a complex phenomenon, of international and interdisciplinary importance, which touches on economic, mathematical, jurisprudential, political and social issues.

The interest in cryptocurrencies has manifested itself both with regards to "blockchain" technology, and for the possibility of making payments without the intermediation of third parties (banks and financial intermediaries in general). The evolution of this market, however, must be inextricably linked to a financial investment context.

The interest in this "world" was amplified by the global economic-financial situation, characterized by particularly low interest rates, and due to the

1

expansionary monetary policies adopted by the Central Banks in response to the 2007 crisis. A situation like this has led investors to be more demanding in seeking alternative finance situations that are capable of satisfying their desire for return. For these reasons, many subjects have seen cryptocurrencies as a "financial product", understood with the more generic meaning of investment opportunities, adequate to meet their needs. After having looked at the historical and systemic context that allowed the birth of the first cryptocurrency, Bitcoin, the aim of this thesis is to analyze the investment possibilities in this market.

First of all, through a theoretical study of the functioning of cryptocurrencies, and secondly in a practical way, through a real investment with the creation of a portfolio.

The first chapter of the thesis deals with the phenomenon of cryptocurrencies, in general at first and then focusing in particular on the Bitcoin technology. Bitcoin, as the first cryptocurrency, deserves special consideration and a more accurate and complete analysis that will be reserved for subsequent cryptocurrencies.

For this reason, all of the issues in the first chapter concerning its functioning, will be touched upon; from the main purpose intended by the creator of Bitcoin Satoshi Nakamoto, to the revolutionary technology of the blockchain. Particular attention will also be paid to those who work for the operation of the Bitcoin network, the so-called "Miners", and for those who allow the exchange of cryptocurrencies into fiat currencies and vice versa, the so-called "exchanges", right up to where Bitcoin is held in the various types of wallets (wallets).

The second chapter deals with introducing and classifying cryptocurrencies that were developed after Bitcoin. The classification is carried out both by taking into account the objective pursued by the developers and creators of the "coins", and by studying the peculiarities of the technology underlying the cryptocurrencies. An analysis of the market trend as well as a comparison with Bitcoin, will also be presented for each cryptocurrency, in order to identify the differences. The choice of Bitcoin as a reference and comparison "coin" is undoubtedly linked to the fact that it is still the most important and well-known cryptocurrency. As well as the one that dominates (in technical terms precisely the "dominance") the sector from the point of view of the capitalization market.

CHAPTER 1
CRYPTOCURRENCIES AND BITCOIN

I n recent years, a payment system has emerged that is closely linked to information technology and the web network. The Internet was the most important innovation that involved the 20th century in a way that influenced all aspects of reality. A general change in social, economic, political and legal has taken place on the large scale of everyday life, with a gradual and disruptive infiltration.

In this constantly evolving context, banks have also had to adapt to changes, updating and sometimes revolutionizing their payment systems, in order to make them more effective and efficient in allowing quick and secure online transactions.

The world of payment systems and finance is transforming before our eyes. Digitized resources and channels, new financial instruments and systems are creating new methodologies for financial transactions and capital investments. Cryptocurrencies, also known as virtual currencies, are part of this process of innovation and technological adaptation.

WHAT ARE CRYPTOCURRENCIES?

Bitcoin has been in use since January 2009, and was the first cryptocurrency. The second cryptocurrency, Namecoin, emerged only two years later, in April 2011. Since then, thousands of virtual currencies have emerged, and hundreds of them can be traded on exchanges and have a considerable value and market capitalization.

The answer to the question of what cryptocurrencies are is neither simple nor trivial. A cryptocurrency is a cryptographic asset (asset, in the broadest meaning of the term), in the sense that it uses cryptography to guarantee the security of its transactions, of a digital type, which is used as an exchange asset between subjects operating in the network. It is said that cryptocurrencies are generic "assets" because from the current regulation and their usage, it is not yet possible to specifically establish which category of assets they fall into. On the one hand, cryptocurrencies may seem like assets similar to "coins", as they are used for the

6

purchase of other assets. On the other hand, as will be analyzed later in the thesis, they have characteristics and uses similar to those of financial assets, in the sense that they are put into circulation by companies, as means for financing the companies themselves; a function similar to the share market, without allowing those who buy them to become owners (shareholders) of the company in question.

The common element of these different virtual currencies is precisely the blockchain technology, a public "ledger" that allows users to participate in the network and manage it in the absence of a central authority. The wide potential of application of the blockchain, in various disciplinary areas, is perhaps the aspect that has aroused the most interest in the events that have brought cryptocurrencies to the fore.

Virtual currencies are digital, equal and decentralized. Decentralization lies in the fact that, unlike all traditional currencies, cryptocurrencies do not have a central body that deals with their issue, there is no Central Bank that controls its value and no intermediaries that are required for the validation of transactions. Cryptocurrencies use cryptographic principles for the validation of operations, and for the creation of the money itself; carried out through a process of small but continuous "monetary expansion" over time. The joint process of "creation" of the cryptocurrency and validation of operations, is carried out thanks to the work of the "miners", their task will be further analyzed in a later chapter.

Given the historical location of their advent, it can be said that cryptocurrencies are a response both to the financial and economic crisis that began in 2007, and the need for a unit of account is linked directly to the interconnected world.

The main innovation of cryptocurrencies concerns being able to use the principles of cryptography with a digital currency whose amount is limited. Although bitcoin only started operating at the beginning of 2009, the concept of cryptocurrency has more distant origins, and has developed over time in a progressive manner, taking advantage of new technologies and needs born following the development of the Internet.

First of all, it is appropriate to identify the common

aspects that bind all virtual currencies and retrace the history that led to the birth in 2008 , and the use of it starting from 2009 of the first cryptocurrency: bitcoin.

CRYPTOCURRENCIES IN BRIEF

A first linguistic misunderstanding that needs to be clarified, is the difference between the concept of electronic money (through which an electronic payment is made), and that of cryptocurrency (digital money). The two terms may seem synonymous but in reality they are not at all. When we talk about electronic money or currency,we are referring to what in English is called ecash. The term concerns the currency that is used on the web to make payments, which takes place through legal tender currencies.

Purchases that take place on the web require an electronic payment, a payment without the physical transfer of money. The operation of these transactions is essentially similar for all companies that deal with these type of payments. Firstly, a deposit account is opened and an amount of physical money is paid in with an intermediary. Through the account you can make payments via the Internet in all stores on the web. Each time a payment is made, the amount spent online is deducted from the deposit, and the company transfers it to the recipient's account. Using electronic money is essentially equivalent to making payments through the use of dematerialized fiat money, without the need for an actual passage between those who carry out the transaction.

Cryptocurrencies are the first form of "digital cash", they combine the advantages of electronic money and cash. Like a bank transfer, they allow remote payments; but at the same time, similar to a payment made in cash, they guarantee the instantaneousness of the operation and involve no costs for either, the person making the payment or the person receiving it.

Cryptocurrencies, like a banknote, are anonymous; that is, they do not require the identities of those carrying out the transaction, or the cause of the payment to be disclosed. But, being digital and divisible almost indefinitely, they allow transfers for any amount, from the payment of a few cents, to the regulation of international commercial traffic. Like a payment card, they allow you to pay any amount in real time and securely anywhere in the world. However, in analogy with cash, they allow the subjects carrying out the transaction to remain anonymous.

THE CONCEPT OF CRYPTOCURRENCY

The first person to talk about cryptocurrencies was David Lee Chaum in 1982, when he published an article entitled "Blind Signatures for Untraceable Payments", here he introduced the concept of virtual currency. The publication was not successful at first, probably because the times were not yet ready, and for a long time it was neglected and associated mostly with the chyperpunk movement.

In 1990 Chaum founded the company Digicash in Amsterdam in the Netherlands, who were chosen for their advantageous legislative structure for this type of activity. Digicash aspired to integrate cryptography with money, pursuing the aim of making transactions anonymous. In 1994, thanks to Digicash, the first electronic payment was made. Despite the positive start, the company closed in 1999 due to economic problems. Although he was the first to introduce the concept of cryptocurrency, Chaum with his company did not develop one, but dealt with electronic money.

SATOSHI NAKAMOTO, THE BITCOIN

Satoshi Nakamoto's article, referred to in the previous paragraph, talks about a decentralized and purely peer-to-peer virtual currency (PTP or P2P) that allows online payments without going through an intermediary.

The expression PTP indicates a logical architecture model of a computer network, whose nodes are arranged in hierarchical order through equal forms. which Designed to act as both server and customer (client or fixed server) to the other end nodes of the network. The key thing that sets this network apart is that every node is able to initiate or complete a transaction.

Decentralization lies in the fact that in bitcoin, unlike other traditional currencies, there is no central body that controls and manages the issue, regulating the functioning and work of those who perform the function of intermediaries.

The European Central Bank (ECB) is the central body that controls the euro through a monetary policy in the countries of the Euro Zone; similarly, the Federal Reserve (Fed) control the US dollar. For bitcoin, on the other hand, there is no subject, be it a public body or a private body, to perform this function. Despite this, saying that the Bitcoin network has no control is profoundly wrong, in fact control exists. It is widespread (in the sense that it is shared among the network participants), and distributed in the network, guaranteed by adherence to a common protocol.

The protocol is formed by a set of rules that define the functioning of the system, and that apply in the functioning of the Bitcoin software. All hardware devices in which the Bitcoin software operates (technically defined as "network nodes"), can communicate through the network with other devices, thus actively managing the cryptocurrency. The greater the number of nodes joining the network, the more the "decentralization" becomes significant and effective.

Since the software and protocol were conceived and released by the inventor of Bitcoin (Satoshi Nakamoto), some skeptics think that the "control" and central authority of the currency is in the hands of the creator himself. This however is disproved by the nature of the Bitcoin project being an open-source as well as the software being "open" to developers who want to make improvements. However, it is impossible for the developers themselves to force a drastic change to the software, as each node can freely choose which version of the software to use, provided that it is compliant and compatible with the software used by the other nodes. Basically, the consent between users and developers of the system is necessary for it to function properly.

To overcome the lack of centralized control, a peer-to-peer network is used and a digital signature is required to complete any cryptocurrency transactions. The P2P network is used to carry out "time stamps" to affix the application of an alphanumeric algorithm. As a reward to the node that first manages to execute the algorithm, a quantity of bitcoin is released, this process in IT terms is called "hash", and essentially consists in the transformation through an injective (noninvertible) function of a sequence of characters of arbitrary length (commonly know as a message) in a predefined length sequence called "hash value" or "message digest".

MAIN CHARACTERISTICS OF THE BITCOIN

Under the European Central Bank directive "Virtual Currency Schemes - A further Analysis" of 2015, bitcoin is defined as an unregulated digital currency used among members of a virtual community. Bitcoin is a virtual currency that is exchanged at any time, with both incoming and outgoing fiat coins (it can be purchased with fiat coins and transformed into fiat coins).

The main features are:

DECENTRALIZATION:

Bitcoin was neither established nor controlled by any central authority. The transaction control is carried out by many independent subjects (the nodes). In this way the presence of intermediaries is not necessary for the carrying out of cryptocurrency transfers.

INDEPENDENCE AND NON-SUBJECTION TO MONETARY POLICY:

The absence of a central authority means that the circulation of money cannot be increased or decreased at will, such as what occurs in the monetary policy of central banks. The money supply is established a priori by the protocol, it increases in a manner before

decreasing until the maximum threshold of pre-established units of 21 million bitcoins is reached.

The increase in working capital occurs every time an algorithm is executed, in this case through the so-called mining, which makes it possible to operate the system. Each time an algorithm is executed, a reward for this is given to the "miner", that receives in exchange, an amount X of newly issued bitcoins predetermined by the protocol. The quantity X is the commissions of those who carry out transactions in that period. For example, a subject A who transfers 1 bitcoin (BTC in abbreviation) to a subject B, can decide to leave a commission of 0.0001 BTC to the miners. The sum of all the commissions left, is attributed to the miner who first executes the algorithm.

For the first four years after the creation of bitcoin, the amount X decided as a reward for the resolution of the algorithm, was 50 bitcoins. Every 4 years the amount of bitcoin issued after each operation is reduced by 50%. So from 2013 until 2017, the premium for mining was 25 BTC. At this time and for the next 2 years, 12.5 bitcoins will be issued for each execution of the algorithm. The execution of the algorithm occurs every about 10 minutes; this time period is established by the system, and is kept the same because every two weeks, the algorithm is calibrated to ensure that this period of time is respected. As a consequence of this choice, the increase in working capital grows, following a geometric series that tends asymptotically to 21 million.

ANONYMITY:

Transactions take place between "public addresses" from which it is impossible to trace the real natural person who operates through that pseudonym. Public addresses are essentially points of receipt and sending of BTC, which can be assimilated to a sort of banking IBAN.

TRANSPARENCY:

All transactions are recorded in public records that areaccessible to anyone, known as the blockchains. By exploring the blockchains, it is possible to know how many bitcoins a public address may have and also which other address has provided them. Simply put, it is as if every time a bitcoin transaction occurs, that transaction remains forever recorded in the bitcoin itself. Despite this transparency, that will be explained later, it is not possible to reach the natural person from the public key.

LOW TRANSACTION COSTS:

The cost for each operation carried out in bitcoins is free, as each user can decide the amount when carrying out the operation. Despite this freedom, commissions are usually around 0.00001BTC. Making the so-called "donations" to the miners of lower amounts, risky for the actual success of the transaction, especially if there are many operations within the 10 minutes in which you make your own. As miners are responsible for authenticating transactions, they can choose which transactions to include in their block. One block, as will be explained later on, represents a "container" within which all of the bitcoin operations carried out in the considered time frame are entered. Each block can contain a number of limited transactions, where the

18

maximum value is 4200; for this reason transactions with low commissions, can be left until last, if in the period in which they are made there are more than 4200 transactions made through BTC.

Much higher costs are those commissions that are placed by the exchanges that deal with the transformation of the Dollar, Euro and other legal tender currencies into bitcoin and vice versa. Although it should be noted that exchanges take enormous risks when dealing with cryptocurrencies, given the very high volatility that characterizes this market, as well as the lack of clear legislation.

SECURITY AND SPEED OF TRANSACTIONS:

Each bitcoin transaction takes an average of 10 minutes to be made, these transactions are irreversible and are impossible to cancel.

THE BLOCKCHAIN

The Blockchain is the computer equivalent of a public ledger in all Bitcoin transactions that have been performed up to now. It can be thought of as a "chain" formed by a set of "blocks", which in turn are formed by a set of transactions. The "chain" has the characteristic of recording and filing all transactions carried out within the network, without the need for a third party to manage the system. The "ledger" is constantly growing, recording any data relating to all operations.

The data is equipped with a defense mechanism, based on encryption, against tampering or the possibility of modification. Transactions take place continuously in the network, while the blocks are "hooked" to the chain, on an average of every ten minutes. Each block is arranged on the chain in a chronological sequence starting from the original block , the so-called "genesis block".

A block is the current part of the blockchain, it can be seen as a "container" inside of which all transactions awaiting authentication are stored. The number of data that can be entered in each single block is defined and limited, as already mentioned, to a maximum of 4200 transactions; one every seven seconds or so. Each block is filled with accounting records, coinciding with the individual transactions (for example A transfers the number of bitcoins to B), which operate in a similar way

20

to a banking IBAN. Once completed and authenticated, the block is linked to the blockchain and remains permanently recorded in the database (the transaction cannot be canceled in any way). The global network of nodes carries out the chaining every 10 minutes, before the authentication of the new block, it verifies the effective connection of all of the blocks of the chain (all of the blocks from the genesis block up to the last authenticated block).

Through the mechanism just described above, it is possible to verify at any time, that the transactions have taken place correctly, so that each bitcoin is transferred only once, avoiding the so-called "double spending". In this way, the functioning of the blockchain prevents a subject from sending the same bitcoin to two different individuals. Each node (i.e. all computers connected to the Bitcoin network), holds a copy of the blockchain, which is automatically downloaded by each miner who joins the Bitcoin network.

The Blockchain is a system where the smallest particle is the single transaction, the basic accounting entry where the set of several transactions form a block and the set of all the blocks form the chain.

Until a few years ago, the blockchain was used only for the operation of the Bitcoin network, in the sense that all the possible application areas, to which such a technology could have been applied, had not yet been identified. In recent years, however, interest in this technology has increased and there could be many future applications. From this perspective, the birth of many cryptocurrencies should be read, interesting not so much for the currencies themselves, but rather for the technologies that underlie the actual cryptocurrencies. In fact, very often companies that are involved in developing a blockchain "create" their own currency (this will be analyzed in the second chapter).

Blockchain has the same importance and function that IPO30 (Initial Public Offering) have for normal companies; to raise capital to reinvest for the development of the company itself. For this reason, blockchain technology has been met with great interest from financial giants and very often from institutions. This suggests that in the future, the "chain" can be applied in finance (the so-called FINTECH).

Therefore, in the near future, the use of the blockchain could be fundamental for the transmission of information between financial intermediaries, and the various supervisory authorities. On the one hand, leading to facilitating control and compliance procedures and, on the other, to greater efficiency and speed of supervision.

In addition to financial applications, the applications of the blockchain can be many others and move on an interdisciplinary field. Great importance could have an application in contracts in the phenomenon known as REGTECH, contraction of Regulation and Technology, that is the use of technological tools to support the procedures of adjustment, compliance, regulations, laws, reporting.

To better understand how the blockchain works, it is necessary to introduce the concept of "mining" and the function performed by the so-called "miners".

THE BLOCKCHAIN AND CRYPTOGRAPHY

The security of the blockchain comes from the type of cryptography it uses. Each transaction recorded on the blockchain is encrypted and only its recipient is able to decrypt it. In this way, the blockchain does not need to implement particular security systems to "defend" a data, as this is made indecipherable by all those who are not authorized to do so. This was made possible by employing asymmetric cryptography.

HOW DOES ASYMMETRIC ENCRYPTION WORK?

Asymmetric cryptography is based on the use of a pair of keys: a public key and a private key. The key pair is mathematically linked by a function, this ensures that a message encrypted with one of the two keys can only be decrypted by the other.

Let's take an example to clarify what has just been said. We have two people: A and B. A wants to send a text document to B, but wants to make sure that only B can read the contents of that document. A then decides to use asymmetric cryptography, therefore uses B's public key to encrypt his message (A knows B's public key because, being public, B has made it available to A). The document thus encrypted can no longer be decrypted by A, as it is not in possession of B's private

24

key (this, unlike the public key, is indeed private: only B has it). B receives the document and manages to decrypt it using his private key. Once B has received and opened the document, he decides to reply to A using the same encryption method, so as to be sure that only he can read the contents of his document. It then encrypts the document using A's public key. A receives the document and manages to decrypt it using his private key.

How asymmetric encryption works is as simple as it is effective. You should have understood that anyone with the public key used to encrypt a message, will not be able to decrypt it, the only way to do this is to use the private key associated with the public key used. This mechanism is not effective if used in reverse, as if you were to encrypt a message using the private key, anyone with the associated public key would be able to decrypt it.

THE MINING AND THE MINERS

"Miners" play a crucial role in any cryptocurrency system. They are the subjects that allow the operation of the Bitcoin network and, through their active participation, guarantee the security of the protocol. Miners are responsible for grouping and authenticating transactions that take place via bitcoin. Their activity consists in solving the "hashes" for the authentication of transactions and operations, therefore they have a function of "notaries", in the sense that they certify the validity of the bitcoin transfer procedures, by creating new blocks to add to the " ledger "(the blockchain).

The miners also provide the computing power necessary to protect the blockchain from possible attempts to subvert and centralize its operation. New blocks are added at constant times. To guarantee the timing, the protocol provides that the difficulty of solving the hashes depends on the number of subjects that are involved in the mining. Regardless of how many transactions take place in the system, every two weeks, according to the Bitcoin protocol, on average 2016 new blocks must be produced, about 1 every 10 minutes, even if no one carries out any transactions. Every two weeks, if the new blocks produced deviate from the target number of 2016, the production difficulty of a new block is revised up or down, depending on whether the output of new blocks was lower or higher to 2016. The difficulty of producing the block depends on the ease with which the hash function can be performed.

If the number of subjects increases, the difficulty of solving the hash increases accordingly, because by increasing the computer power, the miners involved in solving a hash will take less time to find the solution. Since the Bitcoin operation requires that the solutions are "found" every 10 minutes, it is necessary that the hash is adequate for the number of participants in the operations of applying the hash function. The correct solution for the continuation of the blockchain is selected by the protocol, and as a reward for its generation, the miner who solved it receives X amount of new generation bitcoins, plus the sum of all the commissions that have been affixed in block operations.

The commissions, while free, must have an adequate amount. In fact, miners can decide which transactions to enter in the authentication, given that the protocol has a maximum number of authentications with a single validation operation (about 4200 transactions). Presumably miners will choose to authenticate trades with more generous fees first. This way a fee of less than 0.00001 BTC risks taking a longer time to authenticate. The payment of a "prize" reserved for the miners who support the network, was designed to discourage attempts at centralizing the system, which would only be possible with the consent of the majority of the platform participants. Since there is a reward for their work, it is convenient for the miners not to subvert the system and continue to work for its maintenance.

In the beginning, mining could be done with a normal computer. However, as the number of participants in the network increases, this function can only be performed with expensive and sophisticated machinery, designed and created specifically to perform this function. Nowadays, in reality, not even these types of devices guarantee efficiency in resolving hashes. The energy cost to power this type of tool is considerable, for this reason very often the minators come together to increase the probability of being able to solve the hashes and continue the blockchain. The so-called "mining pool" was born from the everincreasing difficulty of being able to "mine" efficiently.

In fact, mining of the most important crypto is now almost an exclusive of mining "giants". These are groups of miners organized with the aim of dividing the computational capacity to be able to execute the various hashes of cryptocurrencies with higher probability.

WALLETS

Bitcoin wallets are similar to a checking account. They provide information at all times regarding the "content" of the wallet and the entry and exit operations in the wallet, as a sort of account statement in real time. Despite this similarity with current accounts, bitcoins are not really contained within the wallet, but are stored in a public register (the blockchain) under specific addresses belonging to different users. The addresses are receiving and sending points consisting essentially of alphanumeric codes of 33 or 34 characters, the first of which is always a "1".

Each code does not contain any information regarding the customer, and being one random combination of numbers and letters, it cannot in any way refer to the user. This feature makes Bitcoin a completely anonymous payment method, through which users make payments with pseudonyms.

Bitcoin transactions are based on the mechanism of "asymmetric transactions", also called public key mechanism - private key. The two keys are alphanumeric codes through which it is possible to perform operations on the Bitcoin platform. Each user holds a pair of keys, one public and one private. The addresses mentioned earlier, derive algorithmically from public keys, which in turn derive through a non-injective function from private keys. Basically, with this mechanism you can get from the private key to the public one, but not vice versa. From the public key, it is impossible to reach the private one; in this sense the transaction mechanism is defined asymmetric. Through the mechanism just described, starting from the address it is impossible to reach the original keys (both the public key or the private key) and consequently the user of the wallet.

The user is authorized to use the bitcoins present in their wallet only at the moment in which it is in possession of its private reference key. It is therefore necessary that the private key must be kept with the utmost confidentiality and not be lost. Each time a new wallet is generated, one hundred (100) public keys are created, that refer to a single private key (kay-pool). This way, the user can take advantage of 100 different addresses connected to the same wallet. Privacy is guaranteed through this mechanism because, even if someone were able to associate a subject with a public key (which is very difficult), it would be impossible for them to trace the other operations carried out by the same subject, as any other movement could be carried out with another 99 keys.

Although this type of operation may seem complex, in reality they are carried out entirely by the system. The wallet is, in fact, quite simple and intuitive and does not differ much from a reserved area of a bank website.

It is possible to have different types of wallets which depend on the level of practicality and safety that the user wants to have. The first wallet, the most common one, is the "desktop wallet". It consists of software being installed on your computer. This type of wallet can be risky, if you do not pay due attention by entering periodically changed passwords, and having an updated antivirus system, your computer could be hacked. In this way it would be possible to recover the private key and therefore steal the bitcoins held in the wallet.

The "mobile wallet" is similar to the "desktop wallet", the only difference is that it is installed as an application on your smartphone. The same goes for the "tablet wallet" which, as is evident from the name, will be installed on your tablet.

Some argue that this is the riskiest way, but perhaps more practical and faster. Other's advise to keep your bitcoins through the online wallet. This type of service is usually provided by exchanges, the online trading platforms that deal with exchanging bitcoin and other cryptocurrencies with fiat currency. As there have been some cases of attacks on exchange platform servers, holding bitcoin online is strongly discouraged.

The last category of wallet is the hardware one; it consists of a device created specifically to keep the private keys of bitcoin addresses and other crypto. This type of wallet connects to the computer via USB (usually a USB stick or hard drive), and thus interact with the wallet software in total safety. Once the operation has been carried out, the hardware wallet can be extracted from the computer device. In this way it will not be possible for any hacker to enter the wallet, being a wallet disconnected from the network. This method of "conservation" of the bitcoin wallet, although less practical to use, is undoubtedly the safest, and gives the user the certainty that their bitcoins are not stolen.

A research study, conducted by the University of Cambridge for the "Alternative Finance" department in September in 2020 by Garrick Hilleman & Michel Rauchs, found that the use of wallets on phones, is the most frequent with 65% of users holding their own cryptocurrencies in this type of wallet, in comparison to only 23% who use hardware wallets (the safest method for holding cryptocurrencies).

MOBILE WALLET	65%
DESKTOP WALLET	42%
WEB WALLET	38%
TABLET WALLET	31%
HARDWARE WALLET	23%

While it may seem like a trivial statistic, it is not at

all. Such a distributed use of portfolios may lead us to think, as the Cambridge researchers also underlined, that the interest in cryptocurrencies is to be framed in speculative and financial investment operations. In fact, holding cryptocurrencies in a "mobile wallet", allows users to be able to sell and buy them more quickly than other systems, which are considered safer. As will be analyzed later in the manuscript, the use of cryptocurrencies has taken a different turn than the one that the creator of Bitcoin had originally thought. In fact, they are considered by users to be "financial products", in the broadest sense of the term, ie they are perceived as an investment opportunity.

THE EXCHANGES

To operate through cryptocurrencies, it is almost always necessary to go through bitcoins, which are recognized by all as the most important and most liquid crypto, recommended as the easiest way to transform into fiat money. The purchase of bitcoins can take place in two ways; either through a direct exchange between a subject who holds bitcoins, wants to sell them and who wants to buy them, or through the intermediation of an exchange.

Direct exchange can also be organized through sites which can consequently be considered exchanges, dealing with putting in contact those who are interested in selling or buying bitcoins. The exchange can take place both online, through payments with bank transfers, or through meetings and electronic payments in physical presence.

The meetings obviously take place in places with internet connection and are often organized by the same site. As for the localbitcoins.com site, it is active in 15962 cities and 248 countries, including Italy, making it the leading site in the sector.

The sites that deal with exchanges in physical presence between subjects in Italy, have numerous locations; especially in the north, where they are present in almost all of the former provincial capitals. The cities with multiple locations are: Milan, Turin and Rome.

In any case, the most common way to buy and sell your bitcoins remains to rely on an online intermediary, the real exchange. The exchanges provide services for the trading of cryptocurrencies with legal tender currencies. The role of exchange is fundamental for the virtual currency market, because they guarantee a market for trading and its liquidity and consequently the possibility of creating a price for the various crypto. They essentially have a function of a Market Maker, that is that of an intermediary who "decides" what the prices should be of a purchase and sale of a specific asset.

Exchanges were the first phenomenon that developed following the birth of bitcoin. The first, "Bitcoin Market", was opened on February 6, 2010, since then hundreds of them have been born and the exchange sector is the most important in terms of volumes and activity.

Exchanges can be divided into two groups; those that operate mainly through bitcoins and those that allow a quick transition from various cryptocurrencies to fiat currencies. The former allow the exchange of bitcoins in all other cryptocurrencies, and the person who intends to operate there must therefore own bitcoins and pay them into the exchange account. Once the bitcoins have been deposited in the exchange account, they will be able to purchase all of the cryptocurrencies supported by the platform through bitcoins.

Taking an example; if Luigi wants to buy X units of Litecoin in an exchange that operates only through Bitcoins, he will have to hold enough bitcoins in his exchange account to buy the desired Litecoin. The exchange therefore takes place between Bitcoin and Litecoin. If Luigi wanted to buy another crypto with his Litecoins, he would have to change those Litecoins into Bitcoins and then with Bitcoins buy the desired cryptocurrency. Even if Luigi wants to exchange his Litecoin for fiat currency (dollar or euro), he should first switch to Bitcoins.

When making a cryptocurrency exchange, commissions will obviously be provided for. The use of Bitcoin as a cryptocurrency is due to the fact that Bitcoin is the best known cryptocurrency, with a higher market capitalization and higher liquidity. In other exchanges, it is instead possible to go directly from fiat currency (dollar more commonly or in some cases even euro) to cryptocurrency and vice versa.

KIND OF ACTIVITY'	DESCRIPTION
Order-Book Exchange	Platform that matches users' purchase and sales orders. It can also facilitate the physical meeting of subjects and the direct exchange of cryptocurrencies.
Brokerage Service	Service that allows users to acquire and / or sell cryptocurrencies at a given price.
Trading Platform	Platform that allows you to buy cryptocurrencies or ETFs of the same, even in leverage. The user works only with the platform, there are no operations between users.

The Order-Book Exchange does not buy cryptocurrencies on its own, but combines buy and sell orders, their income derives solely from commissions. In essence, the exchange does not expose itself in the first person in the purchase and sale of cryptocurrencies, the transaction is carried out by the two subjects directly. The intermediary only makes them "meet". This type of function can also be aimed at the physical meeting of people who want to exchange cryptocurrencies, in the way that has been explained above.

The "Brokerage Service" is the real "Broker" function. The intermediary receives a buy and sell order from the user and "goes to the market" to execute it. Also in this case, the risk is minimal and the gain comes from commissions.

The last type of exchange is the more risky one, the "Trading Platform" hold cryptocurrencies in their wallets and make the purchase or sale as a direct seller or buyer of the customer. The platform is one of the two parties carrying out the operation (either the seller or the buyer). In this last case of exchange, the platform assumes a very high risk, because it exposes itself to the possibility that cryptocurrencies depreciate or revalue; the risk is furthermore accentuated by the very high volatility that characterizes the cryptocurrency market. From this perspective, the considerable commissions required in each operation should be read.Here they are around 3.5% for each operation, both for purchase and sale. In addition to a higher purchase or sale price, in the case of purchase, or lower.

After having identified and briefly analyzed the world of cryptocurrencies, dwelling on the pivotal moments of their birth and on the characteristics of the first cryptocurrency, Bitcoin, the goal of the next chapter will be to select and explain the distinctive features of the main cryptocurrencies that are traded in the market right now. It is necessary to focus on them to analyze the technological innovations they have developed with respect to Bitcoin, and in particular the innovations regarding the blockchain. As explained later, other blockchain technologies have arisen which, although starting from the same assumptions, differ substantially from the technology that is the basis of Bitcoin, and have had considerable interest in the potential areas of application to which they can be adapted.

CHAPTER 2

THE MAIN CRYPTOCURRENCIES

T he main feature of the Bitcoin project is that it is open-source, to allow anyone participating in the network to introduce improvements to the platform. While on the one hand, this feature was one of its strengths, through which it was possible to continuously improve and make the network more efficient with the contribution of developers from all over the world, on the other hand, it proved to be a weakness because it has made it possible to create new cryptocurrencies competing with BTC; which, in a different way, exploited the public information underlying the Bitcoin platform.

The cryptocurrencies created after Bitcoin, can be divided into three groups: the "Altcoins" (or "Alternative Coins", alternatives to Bitcoin), the "Innovative Cryptocurrencies" and the "Cryptocurrency platforms". The former are developed either directly by Bitcoin with a "fork" of the project, that is an "expansion" of a new software project that starts from the source code of an existing one (in this case from that of Bitcoin), or they are developed from the beginning, retracing or even copying, almost entirely the BTC protocol.

The Altcoins therefore can be described as cryptocurrencies that do not introduce substantial or important innovations, to either the Bitcoin procedure or the blockchain; they are basically copies of Bitcoin. Hundreds of examples of altcoins can be found. To name a few, we can mention: "Namecoin" the second cryptocurrency, born from a fork of Bitcoin in April 2011, "Dogecoin", "Dash" or the more recent "Bitcoin Cash". As already mentioned, Altcoins do not present substantial improvements to Bitcoin, but some of them have the objective of overcoming some shortcomings of Bitcoin technology, from the point of view of efficiency. Just to give an example, the times required for a Bitcoin transfer are relatively long if we consider those used by cryptocurrencies born later.

The "Innovative Cryptocurrencies", unlike the Altcoin, are virtual currencies whose operation,

42

although starting from the principles of Bitcoin, is innovative. The innovation may lie in the fact that the blockchain is conceived in a different way, as in the case of "Iota", or other characteristics of the cryptocurrency may differ substantially. This is the case of "Ripple" which, for example, is a centralized cryptocurrency, in the sense that it is controlled by a central third party.

Finally, the "Cryptocurrency platforms", such as "Ethereum", explained later, allow the creation of "smart contracts". Ethereum is the second largest cryptocurrency by market capitalization after Bitcoin, and is considered, due to the substantial innovation it has introduced, as a 2.0 cryptocurrency. The substantial innovation of Ethereum lies in the fact that, in addition to being a cryptocurrency, it is also a platform within which "applications" can be developed and can run other cryptocurrencies.

All cryptocurrencies are a platform (even Bitcoin is), but such a platform can be used exclusively for transactions that take place through the cryptocurrency that was born on that specific platform. The "Cryptocurrencies 2.0", on the other hand, have a platform programmed to be shared with those who want to use it It is therefore used for both, the transactions of the main cryptocurrency of the platform, and as a platform suitable for exercising the functions described above. The functioning of the Ethereum platform and of the cryptocurrency 2.0 platforms in general will be explained later in this chapter.

In addition to the distinction made above, a further differentiation of crypto must be introduced, based no longer on the underlying technology, but on the platform on which they operate. From this point of view, there are two types of cryptocurrencies: "Coins" and "Tokens". The "Coins" are independent cryptocurrencies, whose functioning does not depend on any other cryptocurrency, they have their own blockchain and their own network. The "Tokens", on the contrary, are cryptocurrencies that operate on the same platform as a "Coin", and substantially depend directly on that "Coin". Tokens do not have their own blockchain or platform, but are developed within the blockchain and the platform of a Coin. This type of cryptocurrency can only be developed within a cryptocurrency 2.0 platform, i.e. crypto such as Ethereum or NEO.

Just to give an example, consider the NEO cryptocurrency, which will be covered later. Those who own NEO, are assigned a proportional amount of another crypto, NEO's "Token", the "GAS" to predefine periods of time. Therefore, with mechanisms like this, a sort of "dividend" in the form of another cryptocurrency "Token" than the one held, is attributed to the owner of a specific crypto. Other Tokens, running within the platform of a Coin, can be developed independently from the Coin; without being generated and provided as a "dividend" to the holders of the main Coin of the platform. An example of this can be EOS, the most important Token in terms of market capitalization, which was developed in the Ethereum platform, but independently of the Coin Ethereum. The platform that has the most success for its Token operation is undoubtedly Ethereum. If you visit the sitehttps://coinmarketcap.com/tokens/, eight of the first ten tokens based on the market capitalization "run" on the platform Ethereum.

Summarizing what has been said so far, cryptocurrencies differ in terms of innovative scope compared to Bitcoin in; "Altcoin", "Innovative cryptocurrencies" and "Platform cryptocurrencies". In turn, the "innovative cryptocurrencies" can be innovative in two respects: 1) in regards to the functioning of the blockchain, for example Iota and 2) in regards to the fundamental characteristic of decentralization, such as the case of Ripple which is a centralized crypto.

The last category is that of "Cryptocurrencies 2.0", for example Ethereum and NEO; as mentioned, they are not only cryptocurrencies but are also platforms within which it is possible to operate and develop "smart contracts", applications and other cryptocurrencies (the so-called Tokens). Cryptocurrencies operating within platforms of another cryptocurrency differ from regular cryptocurrencies. Traditional cryptocurrencies are defined as "Coin", ie those that have their own blockchain and their own platform within which they can operate independently. Whilst other, cryptocurrencies that work through a platform of others such as cryptocurrencies 2.0, are defined as "tokens", and therefore appear to be dependent on this platform.

Considering the turmoil that rages in the crypto world, I believe it is necessary to analyze the categories of cryptocurrencies one at a time, explaining their characteristics. For each crypto category analyzed, the main cryptocurrencies belonging to this category will also be studied.

CHARACTERISTICS OF CRYPTOCURRENCIES

Before proceeding with the explanation of the categories of cryptocurrencies, it is useful to introduce some fundamental concepts that will be used to analyze the various cryptocurrencies. First of all, it must be said that from here on all the data used and the information regarding market prices, market capitalization, trading volume, etc ... will refer to what is reported by the sitecoinmarketcap.com/. The choice of the site, the most authoritative and complete among those dealing with the cryptocurrency market, was almost mandatory. In fact, this site is the only one that provides information for approximately all of the 1500 cryptocurrencies existing at this time. Even the Bloomberg platform, despite having been consulted for some comparisons and researches, does not provide the information on the cryptocurrencies considered in this book, with the same punctuality and completeness.

MARKET CAPITALIZATION

The first concept that will be used for the analysis of cryptocurrencies, is that of "Market Cap".

The market capitalization of the cryptocurrency is calculated by multiplying the number of units of cryptocurrency, in circulation with the average market price of that crypto.

It is possible to draw a parallel in this sense, with the market capitalization of shares traded on regulated markets. The market capitalization of cryptocurrencies is calculated in a similar way; in this sense, there is a tendency to equate cryptocurrencies with financial instruments used as shares. As will be later discussed, in reality, cryptocurrencies are by no means shares of the companies that issue them. Those who hold a cryptocurrency, in fact do not become the owners of that company, but simply own an "asset" issued by the company itself. This asset, however, is different from all assets known by law. It is neither a share, nor a bond, nor a hybrid financial instrument.

VOLUME OF TRADE

The volumes represent the set of trading operations carried out on a cryptocurrency in a given unit of time. With reference to securities traded on the regulated market, and consequently also to cryptocurrencies, volumes can be interpreted as the expression of the interest that investors place in a particular security or market.

The volumes are also an indicator in regards to the dynamism of the market and also provide information on the relationship that exists between supply and demand. In addition to this, the analysis of the market volume is interesting for the study of cryptocurrencies, because it provides an approximate indication of the liquidity of the digital currency in question.

According to technical analysts, volume is a measure

of the intensity or pressure that underlies a trend. The higher the volume, the more reliable and lasting the trend will be. Some financial market observers attribute to these "physical" behaviors, imagining that the trajectories followed by prices on the chart are governed by laws similar to those that regulate the movement of a body in real space. Hence the belief that volumes, or rather their increase, is of greater importance in the early stages of an uptrend rather than a bearish one. The analysis of the trend of volumes can therefore provide a series of important signals of confirmation or uncertainty of the trend.

CIRCULATING SUPPLY

The last characteristic that will be considered is the currency in circulation. It indicates the number of cryptocurrency that has been issued. The most important feature of most cryptocurrencies is that they have a limited number of units that can be issued. For this reason, it is certainly important to take into account the amount of currency already issued; the closer you are to the maximum number envisaged for the cryptocurrency, the more you may be led to think that the value of the cryptocurrency can increase (and the asset is limited).

In a similar way, the maximum value of cryptocurrency units that can be reached must also be analyzed; the lower this number is, the more it is likely that the value of the cryptocurrency can be high (obviously the price depends above all on the validity and reliability of the cryptocurrency project in question and the trust that the market places on this project).

If we consider cryptocurrencies that have a very high circulation, the price per single cryptocurrency will tend to be lower. On the contrary, when a cryptocurrency has a low number of circulation its price will tend to be high. The working capital must therefore be assessed with two precautions; the first is to evaluate it in absolute value. (If the currency is "High" or "low" compared to that of other competing cryptocurrencies). Secondly, it must be evaluated in proportion to the maximum circulating available.

These are the three fundamental characteristics from a numerical point of view that can be analyzed in a cryptocurrency. The analysis can be limited only to these three aspects, which in any case are the most significant, above all due to the difficulty in finding other reliable data and for an adequate period of time.

THE ALTCOIN

Since the aim of this thesis is to analyze the possibilities of investing in cryptocurrencies, it is, in my opinion, necessary to identify which are the main "Altcoins", listing their main characteristics, strengths and weaknesses as well as any possible future developments, that could change the price or make it join the most widespread use.

To initially select the most important cryptocurrencies in an approximate way and in order to analyze them, their market capitalization, trading volumes and their presence in the various exchanges, their deal with coins are taken into account. Referring to market capitalization, the most important "Altcoin" is BITCOIN CASH, a cryptocurrency that occupies the fourth place in terms of classification according to market capitalization. The other Altcoins are LITECOIN (in fifth place in the market capitalization ranking), MONERO (in tenth place) and DASH (in

52

eleventh place). All the "Altcoin" cryptocurrencies mentioned here will be examined in the following paragraphs in order of market capitalization.

BITCOIN CASH

Bitcoin Cash, https://www.bitcoincash.org/, was born as a "fork" of Bitcoin on 1 August 2017 (in reality we speak of a "hard fork" given the importance of the fork in question). This cryptocurrency aims to continue the Bitcoin project and overcome some inefficiencies. The developers

decided to make a similar amount of Bitcoin Cash available to everyone who held "Bitcoin" at the time of the fork. The cryptocurrency therefore depends on Bitcoin at its birth. The blockchain of the Bitcoin Cash binds to the Bitcoin Blockchain from the start. In the sense that until August 1, 2017, the blockchain of the two cryptocurrencies is the same, but from August 1, 2017 it starts an independent blockchain and operates completely unrelated to Bitcoin.

Although it was born as a fork of Bitcoin, and has been on the market for a limited period of time (less than a year), Bitcoin Cash immediately managed to reach a considerable price and in fact, quickly placed itself among the first places in cryptocurrencies in regards to market capitalization. Like most cryptocurrencies, Bitcoin Cash (BTCC in acronym) is characterized by considerable market volatility.

Bitcoin Cash is the result of a very long dispute between the programmers and developers of the Bitcoin network, over the overcoming of the so-called "Bitcoin Scalability Problem". The problem refers to the limited amount of transactions that can be made within the Bitcoin network. As already seen in the first chapter, the problem of the limited quantity of transactions that can be processed by the network, is linked to the fact that the blocks in the Bitcoin blockchain have a limited size and frequency, in particular: The dimensional problem concerns that a limited number (4200) of transactions per block can be validated in the Bitcoin network.

The problem of frequency is instead linked to the fact that the Bitcoin system provides for a block to be validated about every 10 minutes. This function is not editable, since it was designed by the creator of Bitcoin to ensure that the units of Bitcoin issued were limited. With the times indicated above, the maximum number of transactions that can be validated every second is 7. This can become a problem when more transactions take place than those that can be validated, because it could cause some transactions to

take a long time to validate, with the theoretical possibility that a transaction may never be.

Bitcoin Cash was basically created to solve this problem, and so all those who were in possession of Bitcoin also became owners of the same amount of Bitcoin Cash.

As happens in all forks, there has been a split in the blockchain which has therefore led to complete independence (from the split date 1 August 2017) between Bitcoin and Bitcoin Cash. The substantial difference lies in the fact that in BTCC each block has a much larger size, which allows you to perform more transactions within it.

LITECOIN

The fifth Altcoin by market capitalization is Litecoin. The cryptocurrency has been distributed since October 7, 2011 and as stated by the main page of its website, is "a decentralized global currency based on Bitcoin technology". Also with regards to the inventors of Litecoin, the aim of the project was to improve the technology of Bitcoin by overcoming some gaps in the latter. Litecoin software was first

deployed in October 2011 on the software project hosting platform "GitHub", by former Google employee, Charles Lee. The main characteristics of Litecoin, which differentiate it from Bitcoin, are the shorter period of time required for the validation of a block, and the significant increase in the number of cryptocurrency units provided by the system.

As for the first Litecoin innovation, it is aimed at solving the problem of the number of transactions that can be validated in each block and the validation duration of a block. By reducing the block validation times, it is possible to obtain an efficiency of the two problems described above.

A different argument must be made for the amount of Litecoin circulating units envisaged by the system. When Bitcoin reached a considerable price level, in terms of fiat currencies, it became increasingly difficult to use it as a means of payment but this problem arose not so much due to the impossibility of dividing Bitcoin as a percentage (Bitcoin is transferable up to the minimum unit of 0.000001).

As observed from the Litecoin site itself, it is a "copy" of Bitcoin. In fact, the site publicly states that the functioning of the cryptocurrency is the same. Litecoin, whose acronym is LTC, is therefore a P2P (peer-to-peer) cryptocurrency that is based on an open source system. Litecoin is currently the second largest virtual currency by market capitalization.

Like all cryptocurrencies, Litecoin is not issued by any central authority, but "comes to life" thanks to mining procedures. Through this activity, the so-called miners solve complex mathematical problems in exchange for cryptocurrencies. This is another of the characteristics that Litecoin has in common with Bitcoin and other virtual currencies in circulation.

The incentive for miners is 50 Litecoin for each successfully verified block. The reward in terms of Litecoin, as in the case of BTC, it halves every 4 years. Every 2.5 minutes, the network generates a so-called block that is added to the others and with them composes the blockchain, the public register of all transactions in Litecoin. As in the case of Bitcoin, the maximum number of Litecoin has already been established by the system and is 84 million.

At the time of the Litecoin's birth, its creator Charles Lee made a comparison between Bitcoin and Litecoin, comparing Bitcoin to gold and Litecoin to silver. This desire for comparison is also evident from the choice of the logos of the two cryptocurrencies; the first in gold color, the second characterized by silver gray. The comparison with gold and silver was made above all, to justify the existence of both cryptocurrencies; the two precious metals have the same safe-haven function and their different price is characterized by their different rarity (Litecoin was also voluntarily made less rare than Bitcoin). Lee wanted to send an important message, namely that of the possibility of coexistence of two very similar cryptocurrencies.

MONERO

Litecoin was the first Altcoin that met with great success and a limelight on an international level, so much so, that starting from 2013 it has often been the protagonist of articles by important newspapers such as the "Wall Street Journal" and "New York Times", which identified it as a possible alternative to Bitcoin, if not actually in some cases as his successor. After the interest that has developed in the world of "Alternative Coins", many programmers started working on and developing other crypto projects.

The programmers of alternative cryptocurrencies have considered it essential, for the development to distinguish each of them with a conceptual or programmatic distinctive trait, which could guarantee a characteristic of exclusivity to the new crypto.

One of these projects, which ended in early 2014, led to the birth of "Monero", XMR in acronym. The cryptocurrency was created starting from April 18, 2014, the most important developers are the Spaniards, Riccardo Spagni and Fransisco Cabañas.

At first the cryptocurrency was called "BitMonero", only later the initial "Bit" was lost to make way for simply "Monero". In the introductory video of the cryptocurrency, the Monero programmers insist on the importance of "Financial Privacy" and on the crypto

60

slogan "You are your own bank".

Monero is a decentralized, digital and secure cryptocurrency, based on cryptographic technology operated by a network of users, whose transactions are confirmed and immutably registered on the crypto blockchain. The three main features of Monero are: security, privacy and non-traceability.

The privacy of cryptocurrency is guaranteed by the fact that the functioning of the blockchain, although similar to that of Bitcoin, is not completely public. The origin, amount and destination of all transactions carried out are obfuscated. Therefore, Monero makes all the characteristics of Bitcoin its own without compromising the privacy and anonymity of transactions. In any case, there is the possibility of cryptographic technology being operated by a network of users whose transactions are confirmed and immutably registered on the crypto blockchain.

Potentially becoming, "Selectively Trasparent", meaning that it may be possible to decide to make one, some or all of their transactions visible, and it can also be chosen which subjects can see those transactions.

DASH

The last "Altcoin" that will be considered in this thesis is Dash. Like Bitcoin, Dash is an open-source peer-to-peer cryptocurrency. Its creator and current CEO is Ryan Taylor, former manager of the US company McKinsey & Company. The digital currency was put into circulation starting from 18 January 2014 with the name of XCoin (XCO). On the 28th of the same month, the name was changed to DarkCoin, only to be changed again in March 2015 to Dash (from the English Digital Cash).

Despite having a similar operation to Bitcoin, Dash has introduced a series of improvements in the operation and speed of transactions.

From an "administrative" point of view, the functions of Dash are different from those of Bitcoin.

There are two functions in the Dash networks; that of "Minatore" and that of "MasterNode". The former perform the same function performed for other cryptocurrencies, namely that of creating blocks and validating transactions that take place in the network. The "MasterNodes" have a different task, they are the ones who deal directly with the "optional functions" of

Dash. The optional functions are in fact additional services that, for a fee, can be requested by those who make transactions through Dash. There are two optional functions: the so-called "Private Send" and "Instant Send". The first function concerns precisely the possibility by the users of the Dash payment services, to carry out their transaction in complete anonymity.

This service takes place by "mixing" several transactions made by subjects who want to use this service. The mechanism consists of Dash's outgoings and revenues from one public address to another. Through this mechanism it will not be possible to trace in any way, who made the individual transactions, also in consideration of the fact that each user has 100 public addresses for each public key and a total of 100 public keys.

"Instant Send" consists of the possibility for those who hold a Wallet Dash to carry out transactions that are authenticated immediately (1.4 seconds on average). These two functions are, as mentioned, guaranteed by the MasterNodes; they are indeed particularly important "knots".

The MasterNodes must be active 24 hours a day and 7 days a week, and to operate they must deposit at least 1000 Dash coins in the system.

The MasterNodes, in addition to the functions described above, have another important function. In fact, by virtue of the large amount of Dash they hold, they have the right to actively participate in the development decisions of the Dash network.

The development of the Dash network works through the financing of projects proposed by users or developers. These projects, which can be presented in a special section of the site, are analyzed and finally put to the vote of the MasterNodes. The projects chosen by the MasterNodes are financed by the network itself and thus allow to improve the functioning of the Dash network. Funding is self-financing as, projects are paid for through the Dash payment to programmers.

Self-financing takes place through a sort of "taxation" of the network, at the time of the creation of a block. When a block is created by miners, the amount of Dash generated by that block is distributed in this way: 45% of the Dash generated is attributed to the miner who solved the hash corresponding to the block, another 45% of the proceeds are distributed to the MasterNodes, as remuneration for the task performed to guarantee the optional functions, and the last 10% is deposited in the "Treasury".

The "Treasury" is a sort of "current account" of the Dash network itself, within which 10% of the Dash generated through the blockchain mechanism converges. The funds contained in the Treasury are spent on remunerating those who propose and develop projects that help improve the Dash network. As mentioned above, the projects are selected by the MasterNodes through a system of "direct democracy" where each MasterNode votes on every decision that must be taken by the network.

CHAPTER 3

INNOVATIVE CYRYPTOCURRENCIES

After analyzing the panorama of Alternative Coins, now we look at innovative cryptocurrencies, i.e. those that have a substantially new characteristic feature in their functioning, compared to Bitcoin. Among them, two of the most important cryptocurrencies can be identified; the first is Ripple and the second is IOTA.

Both are atypical cryptocurrencies, meaning that their fundamental characteristics are unusual and profoundly different from those of normal cryptocurrencies. Ripple stands out for being a centralized cryptocurrency, in the sense that the operation, security and authentication of transactions is managed by a company. IOTA, on the other hand, is profoundly innovative because it does not use the blockchain, but functions through the "Tangle".

RIPPLE

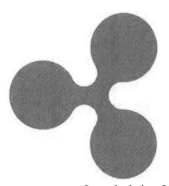

Ripple is a company, founded in 2012 by Ryan Fugger, based in California, that deals with the transfer of assets (understood as fiat currency, gold and other commodities), through its platform. The creation and development of the Ripple platform is the corporate purpose of the company in question and is pursued by the so-called "Ripple Lab" in San Francisco.

The Ripple company was created with the aim of developing a technology that It was designed so it could allow a new real-time payment system, and whose main function was to allow the transfer of funds between banks or financial companies. The company collaborates with a large number of banks, in particular European ones, and has developed a platform that was conceived as a competitor to SWIFT (Society For

Wordwile Interbanck Financial Telecomunication) from which the term "SWIFT bank transfer" is used in technical jargon to mean an interbank and interstate payment.

Although it is only in the initial phase, the collaborations with financial intermediaries are numerous, and are leading to a feasibility study regarding the use of Ripple as a new platform for carrying out interbank transactions.

Another thing is the XRP cryptocurrency, commonly known as Ripple is an atypical digital currency, which many experts in the crypto world do not even consider a cryptocurrency. This foreclosure against XRP is mainly linked to the fact that the digital currency is not decentralized. Although it is based on the blockchain structure, it is controlled by the Ripple company, which develops and guarantees the transactions that take place within its platform.

Another peculiarity of Ripple, which distances it from the world of cryptocurrencies, is precisely the same goal with which it was created. Unlike most cryptocurrencies, XRP was not conceived as a commonly used "coin"; in fact, its function is that "money" that can be used between financial intermediaries, to allow the overcoming and efficiency of old technologies such as SWIFT.

This last feature of Ripple is perhaps the one that moves digital currency the farthest from the "crypto" world and the closest to the world of conventional finance. From this point of view, it can be said that XRP is the first point of conjunction between finance and the world of cryptocurrencies. In a context in which banks and financial institutions very often look to cryptocurrencies as a threat, and as a dangerous source of speculative bubbles, Ripple is the first among cryptocurrencies, that has managed to find concrete interest from financial intermediaries.

XRP has been released since 2012 by the same Ripple company. One of the fundamental characteristics of the cryptocurrency is that all the XRP units envisaged by the system were issued immediately; the expected amount of 100 billion units of XRP was "mined" at the time of the cryptocurrency's birth. The large amount of Ripple mined (if you relate for example to the Bitcoin maximum limit of 21 million), was chosen precisely for reasons of functionality.

The value of Ripple cannot be as high as that of Bitcoin, because the creators did not want XRP to become a virtual store of value (virtual gold) as Bitcoin has become. But they envisioned it could be used in a practical way by Banks for the execution of interbank transactions. If the company's goal of replacing SWIFT technology was met, all banks would like to hold substantial amounts of XRP to sufficiently be able to secure the operations they want to carry out.

IOTA

IOTA is an open-source, non-mineable cryptocurrency project, developed and launched between 2015 and 2016 by a group of German developers. In support of the project, the "IOTA fondation" was founded with the contribution of funds donated by users.

IOTA is an innovative cryptocurrency born with a specific goal; to overcome the burden and heaviness of blockchain technology. As also stated on the official

IOTA website, the developers wanted to operate in the direction of a "lightweight" cryptocurrency.

The inventors of the IOTA started from a very important assumption, namely that in the next decade it is estimated that there will be more than 50 billion devices connected to the Internet. These devices will be connected all over the world, even in countries where banking structures and financial services in general are almost absent.

In addition to the problem of the poor development of the financial economy, these

new countries that are facing the interconnected world, are characterized by inadequate state institutions, which fail to forcefully impose the state currency and which often subject it to strong devaluations. Such weak and highly depreciated coins prevent those who use it from making everyday payments. IOTA has the objective of allowing the management of "micropayments", guaranteeing their safety and having almost zero costs.

Interconnected devices will need to be able to exchange tiny amounts of money with each other, instantly. Precisely for this purpose, IOTA was conceived, which remains suitable for any other scenario in which there is the need to manage any type of transaction, even large ones.

To achieve this ambitious goal, at the time of designing IOTA, it was decided that it must distance itself from blockchain-based cryptocurrencies. While maintaining the vision linked to distributed consensus, a different approach was needed to make the network scalable within the IOTA ecosystem, where there will be tens of billions of connected devices. In fact, from the point of view of IOTA, we want to encourage the use of cryptocurrencies for everyday operations; doing so would have to validate thousands of transactions every second. As previously stated for other cryptocurrencies, including the expansion of blockchain blocks and the reduction of validation times, no cryptocurrency has so far been able to validate more than 200 transactions per second.

IOTA uses the Tangle, which is a software protocol based on direct acyclic graphs that are profoundly different from the blockchain protocol. Before proceeding with the explanation of the substantial innovation of the "Tangle", it is necessary to dwell on the concept of "direct acyclic graph". In computer science, and sometimes in mathematics, we mean by direct acyclic graph, also called "acyclic graph oriented "(from the English Directed Acyclic Graph, DAG), a particular category of graph direct or digraph.

The digraph is the more general structure of a simple tree chart. In a tree chart there is a common source and a set of nodes, positioned in multiple levels. The digraph, unlike the tree chart, does not have such an organized structure, but to each "source", nodes are not ordered in a regular manner. Inside the digraph there are "nodes", or "boxes" of the graph, and "arcs" or the path necessary to get from one node to another.

FEATURES OF IOTA:

No transaction costs: to send an IOTA transaction, the sender's device must verify two previous transactions in the Tangle, performing a "Proof of Work" operation. IOTA lacks the differentiation between "user" and "miner". All the subjects participating in the network are nodes of the IOTA network and must necessarily "work" to be able to participate.

Infinitely scalable: To send a transaction, two more must first be confirmed, and as the number of users increases, the efficiency of the network also increases. This way, the problem of other cryptocurrencies that allow a limited number of operations per second is overcome. The more the network grows, the more IOTA speeds up its transactions. The system adjusts to its size.

Quick transactions: The transaction execution times are inversely proportional to the number of transactions in the Tangle. When IOTA reaches mass adoption, transactions will be virtually instantaneous.

Fixed money supply: All existing units were created in the "genesis block", and that amount will never vary. The total amount corresponds to

2.779.530.283.277.761 iota.

CHAPTER 4

CRYPTOCURRENCIES 2.0

C ryptocurrencies 2.0, also known as "platform" cryptocurrencies, were born from an idea of Vitalik Buterim who is a Canadian programmer, of Russian descent. He is the inventor of Ethereum, which was designed in 2013 when he was just 20 years old. The idea of the Canadian programmer, was to exploit the 360-degree blockchain technology, not limiting its use to the application in the world of cryptocurrencies. Almost parallel to Buterim's idea, another similar operating platform developed, that of NEO.

The platforms are a development of web 3.0 in the sense that they aim to allow the widespread diffusion of the "Smart Economy", through the large-scale development of applications, shared software and smart contracts. The development of the Smart Economy in these platforms is favored by the opensource structure, and in general by the possibility of sharing information among all users. Each application and software can be downloaded for free by users and their scripts are "open" to any person who wants to consult them.

ETHEREUM

Ethereum, unlike Bitcoin, is not just a cryptocurrency; it is a decentralized platform for managing smart contracts. While Bitcoin is intended to serve as a virtual medium of exchange, Ethereum founder Vitalik Burerim did not want to limit his project to just this function. The concept of a platform is much broader than that of cryptocurrency. The Ethereum platform is also a cryptocurrency, the coin that runs in the Ethereum network is precisely the Ether (ETH in acronym), but its main feature is being a platform within which it is possible to develop applications, software and " Smart Contract ". The operation of

these contracts are embodied in the programming of applications that autonomously perform exactly what was programmed at the time of the agreement between the parties. This way there is no possibility of downtime, censorship, fraud or interference from third parties. Buterim's idea, when he started developing Ethereum in

78

2013, was to make the most of all the potential of the blockchain. In fact, he believed that the use of technology as a simple "ledger" for exchanging a cryptocurrency was limiting.

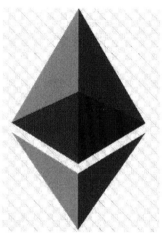

Development of Ethereum began in 2013 and the first version of the software became available starting in February 2014. Since then, a series of software versions have been made public that have introduced and developed three new programming languages for writing Smart Contracts.

To finance the development of the platform, Ether was launched for the first time in a public pre-sale offer, in a form similar to that of IPOs (initial public offerings), which made it possible to raise about $ 19 million in BTC.

In extreme simplicity, Ethereum could be presented as the largest shared computer that is capable of delivering enormous power available everywhere and forever. In other words, Ethereum is a computational platform that is "remunerated" through exchanges that are carried out through Ether. It is a platform that can be adopted by all those who wish to become part of the network and who in this way, will have a solution that allows all participants to have a shared and immutable archive. The Ethereum project is flexible and suitable for use in different application areas, it can be defined as a "Programmable Blockchain" that not only allows you to carry out predefined and standardized "operations", but allows users to create their own "operations".

The basis of the functioning of the entire Ethereum network is the platform's cryptocurrency, Ether. It is used for carrying out all transactions and operations within the platform. For example, a user who wants to "run" his own contract within Ethereum must pay for this service to the system in Ether. Similarly, a developer of an application or software through the platform must "pay" for the service offered by Ethereum. The payment may have either payments of Ether held by the subject, or through the subject's "work"; granting one's computational power to guarantee the Ethereum system.

With regards to the functioning of the Ethereum blockchain, it has the same characteristics as the Bitcoin one: a fundamental function is that performed by the "miners" who create the blocks and validate the transactions. A block is generated every 15 seconds on average, and as a reward for their work, miners receive 15 Ether per Block. The system has not foreseen a maximum number of Ether that can be emitted, for this reason there are currently around 100 million Ether in circulation. The number of Ether, according to what is currently foreseen by the system, will continue to increase constantly, according to the predetermined pattern. However, it cannot be ruled out that programmers may propose a change to the unlimited growth of Ether which, if accepted by the network, could lead to a gradual reduction of their emission, such as the example with Bitcoin.

SMART CONTRACT

The distinctive feature of Ethereum, as well as its most important innovation, is the introduction of "Smart Contracts". Smart contracts are computer protocols that facilitate, verify, or enforce, the negotiation of partial or total execution of a contract. In short, they are contracts that are executed automatically by a system. With contracts of this type, many types of contractual clauses can be made partially or fully automated, self-fulfilling, or both. Smart contracts aspire to ensure greater security than existing contracts and to reduce costs of the transaction associated with bargaining.

The Ethereum platform itself guarantees smart contracts, which is responsible for authorizing, validating and authenticating contracts.

NEO

NEO is the second most important blockchain platform after Ethereum; it is a Chinese developer project, launched shortly after Ethereum in February 2014, which aims to compete with the first platform.

NEO's ambitious goal is to help economic change through the development of the "Smart Economy". The NEO project manages smart contracts and software development on its platform by means of a payment with the platform's coin, the NEO. The platform works through a blockchain whose blocks are generated at intervals of 15 seconds each. The functioning of the network is always guaranteed by the miners, who create and authenticate in blocks and are therefore rewarded for their work with an amount of cryptocurrency.

The NEO programmers, while admitting the similarity of their project compared to the Ethereum one, identify an advantage in terms of scalability, (i.e. the number of operations that can be authenticated by their blockchain every second). An important difference with respect to Ethereum, is that NEO supports various computer languages in common use, such as Microsoft.net and Java. On the other hand, Ethereum requires specific knowledge of its programming languages. Another difference between the NEO and the Ethereum project lies in the quantity of NEO units that can be issued, the limit is set at 100 million units.

FIGURE 2.14119

NEO units are not divisible, in fact it is not possible to buy for example 0.5 NEO. The number of NEOs that can be held must always be an integer. For this reason, for operations within the network, the "GAS" is used as an exchange cryptocurrency, a cryptocurrency subordinate to NEO, but operating in the same network. Anyone who holds NEOs for a certain period of time in their portfolio they receive a quantity of GAS proportional to the amount of NEO held, as if it were a kind of "dividend". In this way, NEO holders have an incentive to hold the cryptocurrency for a long time.

ICO

The ICO (Initial Coin Offering), is a fundraiser through which a "Token" or a "Coin" is offered through a blockchain platform, in exchange for fiat currency or another cryptocurrency (such as Ether, NEO or Bitcoin).

ICOs take place within platforms such as Ethereum and NEO and are implemented through a Smart Contract.Here, a Smart Contract is generated so that the two counterparties are: the company or the person who wants to place the Token or Coin on the market; the person who intends to sign the ICO. Through this contract, the subscriber will receive the cryptocurrency placed on the market at the deadline set by the contract. The proceeds raised through the ICO are used to finance the business or project of those who launched the offer.

The financing mechanism through the ICOs is reminiscent of that carried out by companies that want to go public through the IPO (Initial Public Offering). While similar in scope, the ICO is profoundly different from the initial public offering. Firstly, cryptocurrencies are digital assets, but they do not specifically fall within a financial instrument that is clearly regulated by lawmakers. The parties who are listed to participate in an IPO are protected by the law and have the right not to purchase the newly issued shares until the day the share is actually listed. The most important thing to point out is that when those who participate in an IPO buy the shares of a company; they become shareholders.

The token or coin object of the ICOs can be exchanged and used like a normal cryptocurrency, but their operation and the authentication of their transactions takes place in the same blockchain as the platform on which they are launched.

Those who "launch" the ICO, referred to as "sponsors", usually provide access to a "white paper" describing the project, key team members, and key terms of the ICO (for example, the terms financial statements, contract details and timing).

In the underwriting process, the participant is typically required to transfer cryptocurrency or a fiat currency to one or more designated addresses or the ICO "sponsor" online wallet. Registrations can be completed in minutes. An entity can also be rewarded with ICO tokens by doing some tasks for the issuing company, such as marketing on cryptocurrency forums. Once the ICO is complete, the ICO tokens are distributed to the designated addresses or online wallets of the participants.

CHAPTER 5

INVESTMENTS IN CRYPTOCURRENCIES

The main methods of investing in cryptocurrencies and methods of earning interest on them are briefly described below.

Trading - Through the use of regulated exchanges, it is possible to buy and exchange cryptocurrencies by approaching a global market, open 24 hours a day and 7 days a week. Users have mainly two types of exchange available: centralized (controlled by private companies, where the funds must be sent to the wallets of the exchange itself), and decentralized (the funds remain in the possession of the user and the trading takes place on peer to peer platforms).

The former offer a more similar approach to traditional trading sites, however users may be subject to restrictions based on their country of origin, and they are more prone to hacker attacks. The latter are technically more complex, aimed at an advanced type of user, but offer a greater level of security both in regards to the safeguarding of funds and privacy. Finally, there are other methods to obtain cryptocurrencies quickly, such as swap.

ICOs (Initial Coin Offerings)- They are a crowdfunding category dedicated to Utility Tokens, or cryptocurrencies that through their possession, give access to products or services of a particular company. In the past, subject to strong discussions, they have allowed users to increase the invested capital in a very short time. The increasing exposure of users to this type of offer (investments were sent directly to the teams, without any guarantees), have resulted in the launch of numerous ICO scams.

A greater awareness on the part of users has subsequently made ICOs evolve into IEOs (Initial Exchange Offerings). Briefly, IEOs are similar to ICOs but are managed by large exchanges, which in addition to managing the crowdfunding operation, take the place of users by verifying the legitimacy of the projects presented. Therefore a user who has confidence in the exchange, is more inclined to invest in a project.

STOs (Security Token Offerings) - Are a crowdfunding category dedicated to Security Tokens, or cryptocurrencies that represent real shares of a particular company. This type of offer began to be defined after the regulators expressed their opinion on certain ICOs, defining them as security and not utility. Unlike traditional initiatives, through an STO, it is possible to reach a worldwide audience, through the sale and subsequent trading on a market; which, unlike traditional ones, is open 24 hours a day and 7 days a week. It is worth following the evolution of this type of offer as it could represent the majority of the initiatives that will take place in the future.

Lending - Investors can earn interest on cryptocurrencies through loans. The most common type of lending refers to that of exchanges, where cryptocurrencies are "lent" to traders who request them (borrowers). Most platforms guarantee a 100% return of the loaned capital as well as interest. This type of investment, although aimed at an expert trading audience, is enjoying increasing success thanks to the possibility of earning ever higher interests.

CRYPTO STRATEGIES

Top 10 crypto strategy

This system starts from the assumption that in the Top 10 crypto market capitalization, there is always a "hard core" formed by bitcoin,Ethereum,Litecoin,Bitcoin Cash,Ripple and Dash, while the other positions are quite variable and are traded in turn by coins such as Monero,Iota,Cardano,Ethereum Classic,NEO and NEM.

For example, starting with a budget of $1,000, you have to buy $100 of each of the cryptocurrencies in the top ten.Be sure to check them monthly and cash out when you reach the established goals.

Accumulation Plan Strategy (CAP)

This system was originally applied by banks to investment funds, but it is perfectly replicable also in the world of cryptocurrencies. The basic assumptions of CAPs are the progressive accumulation of capital and the reduction in risk thanks to "dollar cost averaging". Applying it to cryptocurrencies, for example, it is necessary to purchase three different tokens, two perhaps already established, such as bitcoin and Ethereum, and one "emerging", as it can Stellar Lumen. You then decide which sums to invest and how often you have to check the portfolio to see the trend.

Cryptocurrency investment strategy by value

Among the medium / long-term strategies, the "by value" strategy also stands out, which partly resembles the previous one (CAP), but differs in terms of the choice of currencies to bet on.

In this case, cryptocurrencies must be chosen based on their future potential, influenced by values such as; a solid project (see EOS,Verge,Tron), low prices, community of users andthe introduction of any new technologies. Research and analysis on these factors will help you in choosing the right coins for the strategy.

Millesimal cryptocurrency strategy

This is a crypto investment strategy that is based on the analysis of the performance of those tokens that started from a few cents and have made a bang, reaching prices of hundreds of dollars.

We are talking about real "gold nuggets", and your task is to find them among the Top 100. It is advised to select at least five, invest 100 euros in each and keep the investment.

Crypto-trading strategy in the short term

After analyzing strategies indicated for the medium-long term, let's close this roundup with short-term crypto-trading. In this case, the goal is to speculate on the fluctuations that determine the price of an asset every day, or of a crypto in our case.

The strategy requires a lot of time and energy to follow the market, and is based on the simple concept of buying when the price goes down and selling when it goes up.

CHAPTER 6

WHAT ARE THE FIVE STEPS TO SUCCESSFULLY INVEST IN CRYPTOCURRENCIES?

1. Learn the basics

Don't invest in what you don't know! First understand the functioning of the blockchain, the terminology, the technical aspects and the dynamics that are involved in this world.

Don't be rushed, in-depth knowledge of a topic requires a long period of study.

2. Get experience

Crypto markets are quite young and subject to extreme volatility compared to traditional ones. Trading is not improvised and requires experience; you should always only risk an amount that you can afford to lose.

3. Follow the developments in the world of cryptocurrencies on a daily basis.

The world of Blockchain is running faster than any

other traditional sector, so keep up to date with its developments through news sites, social media and by participating in discussion groups on Telegram and other platforms.

4. DYOR - Do Your Own Research

Ensure that you do your research before investing in a project! Check all of the details of the cryptocurrency that you want to invest in, and ask yourself:

What is its capitalization?

What are the market volumes and what is the price history?

Are the people on the team real and verifiable?

Is the business registered according to law?

Is the project popular enough?

Does the whitepaper I am consulting reflect a specific mission, or do the objectives of the project seem unrealistic?

Is the team available to answer my questions and is the community following the project active?

Is the exchange I am using to trade safe and

registered according to the law? And when all this is not enough ...

5. Use your intuition

It's okay to be skeptical. If a project doesn't fully convince you, it may not be worth the investment. If you find that something is wrong or you are not confident enough, perhaps it is time to stop or exit the investment. Immobility is the enemy of a world in constant evolution, so try to inform yourself as much as possible and move in the market according to the knowledge you have acquired and your intuition.

Happy trading!

CONCLUSION

The objective of this guide was to verify the investment possibilities in a complex, non mature and constantly evolving market, such as that of cryptocurrencies. The analysis of the market and the "assets" that compose it was carried out by observing two guidelines. The first was to identify the relevant and distinctive characteristics of cryptocurrencies from a theoretical point of view. This was pursued by explaining the differences between the most important cryptocurrencies and cataloging them.

However, the difficulty of definition and the lack of legislation is not a matter of little interest. In fact, it has an important fiscal repercussion, just think of the taxes on capital gains that should be paid in the event that a cryptocurrency is considered a financial investment. In addition, it should be remembered that if cryptocurrencies were financial investments, considerable information and broader transparency should also be guaranteed, which at this time is not guaranteed at all.

In addition to tax considerations, it must be taken into account that the market of cryptocurrencies and "Blockchains" in general, is very young. The market is not only young but has until recently, been "dominated" in terms of market capitalization by a single "asset": Bitcoin.

To add to these problems, the strong impact that exchanges have on the price of cryptocurrencies, is substantiated in the request for high fees for commissions. This high incidence of commissions is a consequence of the risk to which operators who offer to mediate, in exchanges between fiat currencies and cryptocurrencies are exposed. Such a volatile and poorly regulated market, in fact forces intermediaries to protect themselves and request a profit proportional to the risk taken for the service performed. The situation outlined above is a symptom of non-total market liquidity.

In addition to this, it should be noted that the number of exchanges, although it has greatly increased in the last period, still remains low. The small number does not favour competition, which if it were tougher, would undoubtedly lead to a reduction in commissions.

Printed in Great Britain
by Amazon